DINOSAUR
COLORING BOOK

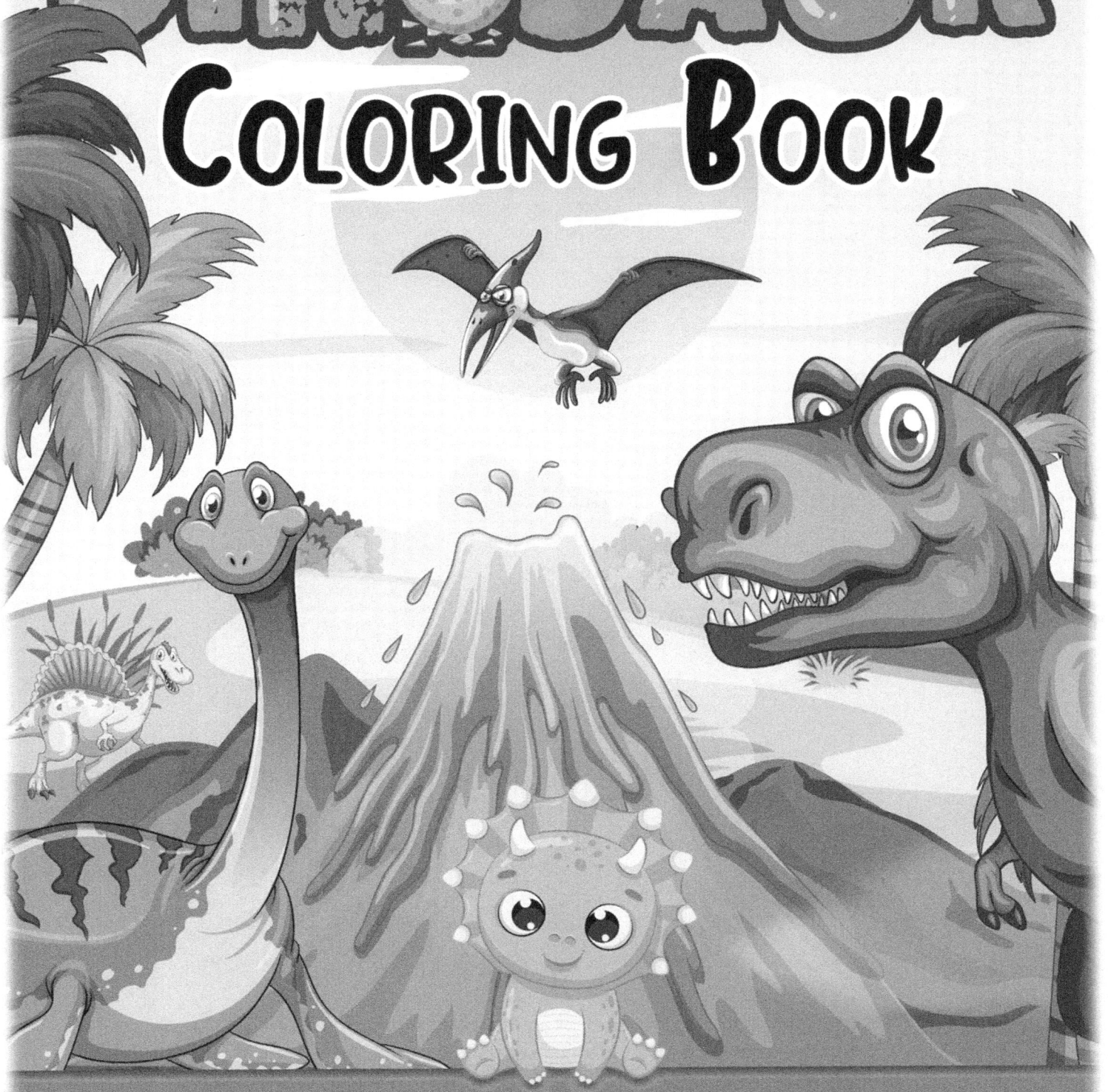

With Fun Facts for Kids!

MW01537891

Copyright © 2020 by Alia Fischer

All rights reserved. This book or any portion therefor may not be reproduced or used in any manner whatsoever without the express written permission of the publisher except for the use of brief quotations in a book review.

First Printing, Sept 2020

ISBN 9798682964918

Author Note

Thank you for purchasing this book. I am confident your little kid(s) will love it and spend hours and hours of fun coloring all the cute pictures that I have designed or purchased from third parties, while learning amazing facts about dinosaurs, which are based on the most up-to-date information out there!

I would love to receive your feedback about this book by submitting a review in the Amazon marketplace from which you purchased it, or by sending me an email to **support@aliafischer.com.**

Amazon reviews are very helpful to better rank books and make them visible to more people, so that buyers can make the best choice by selecting from a larger set of offers.

Moreover, I read all reviews and emails received, and make sure to respond to each email and take your comments / critics into consideration for my next books. I also enjoy reading how people express their satisfaction and how my books have helped them and their children improve their coloring skills while enjoying every moment in the process.

Happy coloring ☺

Alia Fischer

This book belongs to

_____

TRICERATOPS FACTS

Species Type	Ceratops Horridus	**Dinosaur Type**	Ceratopsid
Movement	Quadrupedal (walked on four legs)		
Period	Late Cretaceous Period (around 65 million years ago)		
Diet	Herbivore. Biting off plant material with its beak and processing it with its tooth batteries		
Life Span	40 years		
Dimensions	Could reach up to 9m (30 feet) in length and 3m (10 feet) in height		
Weight	Between 6.5 to 13 tons (Roughly the size of an elephant)		
Found in	United States of America & Canada		
Miscellaneous	Triceratops had 800 teeth at its disposal which allowed it to replace old worn teeth with sharp new ones! The US state of Wyoming has listed it as its state dinosaur since June 1994. A top speed of 35 mph.		

Dinosaurs

Triceratops

TYRANNOSAURUS FACTS

Species Type	Tyrannosaurus Rex	**Dinosaur Type**	Theropod
Movement	Bipedal (walked on two legs)		
Period	Late Cretaceous Period (around 65 million years ago)		
Diet	Carnivore, feasting on the flesh of the animals they caught		
Life Span	Over 40 years		
Dimensions	Up to 13m (43 feet). Among largest carnivorous dinosaurs to ever live		
Weight	Around 16 tons		
Found in	United States of America & Canada		
Miscellaneous	They're known for having 50-60 "banana-sized teeth" that are 30 cm (12 inches) from the root, they could rip 100 kg of flesh in one chomp! They were super smart too, boasting a brain twice as big as those of the other giant carnivores. They could run at speeds up to 25 mph.		

Dinosaurs

Tyrannosaurus

STYRACOSAURUS FACTS

Species Type	Styracosaurus Albertensis	**Dinosaur Type**	Ceratopsia
Movement	Quadrupedal (walked on four legs)		
Period	Cretaceous Period (between 75 and 75.5 million years ago)		
Diet	Herbivore. Ate a wide variety of vegetation near the ground		
Life Span	40 years		
Dimensions	5.5m (18 feet) in length		
Weight	Around 3 tons		
Found in	United States of America (Montana) & Canada (Alberta)		
Miscellaneous	They lived in a terrestrial habitat and reproduced by laying eggs. A notable feature is the six parietal spikes that extended from its neck frill. Can reach a top speed of 35 mph.		

Dinosaurs

Styracosaurus

STEGOSAURUS FACTS

Species Type	Stegosaurus Stenops	**Dinosaur Type**	Thyreophora
Movement	Quadrupedal (walked on four legs)		
Period	Late Jurassic (between 150 and 155 million years ago)		
Diet	Herbivore. Ate a wide variety of vegetation near the ground		
Life Span	Between 75 and 100 years		
Dimensions	Up to 9m (29 feet) in length		
Weight	Between 5 to 7 tons		
Found in	First discovered in 1877 north of Morriso, Colorado, USA.		
Miscellaneous	The state dinosaur of Colorado. Its brain was the size of a walnut. It wasn't an easy meal for predators, as the plates on its back and spiked tail were an excellent way to defend against predators. 30 mph top speed.		

Dinosaurs

Stegosaurus

PTERODACTYL FACTS

Species Type	Pterodactyl Antiquus
Movement	They flew, and also waddled on their back legs and pointed wings
Period	Late Jurassic (between 150 and 155 million years ago)
Diet	Carnivore. Diet most likely consisted of fish and other small animals
Life Span	10 to 25 years
Dimensions	Up to 1m (3.5 feet) wingspan
Weight	Between 2 to 10 pounds
Found in	First discovered in 1784 in the Bavaria region of Germany
Miscellaneous	They had an elongated beak with about 90 razor sharp teeth. They are not actually dinosaurs, they are a pterosaurs and considered a flying reptile.

Dinosaur Type — Pterosaur

Dinosaurs

Pterodactyl

PARASAUROLOPHUS FACTS

Species Type	Parasaurolophus Walkeri	**Dinosaur Type**	Ornithopoda
Movement	Quadrupedal (walked on four legs) and bipedal (walked on two legs)		
Period	Late Cretaceous Period (between 73 and 76.5 million years ago)		
Diet	Herbivore. Ate a wide variety of vegetation		
Life Span	65 years		
Dimensions	10m (31 feet) in Length		
Weight	2.8 tons		
Found in	Discovered in 1920, along the Red Deer River in Alberta, Canada		
Miscellaneous	Had hundreds of teeth that were stacked into multiple rows. As teeth were wore down, new ones would work their way up. The most notable feature is their long, curved cranial crest, that extended back and pointed down towards their shoulders. 30 mph top speed.		

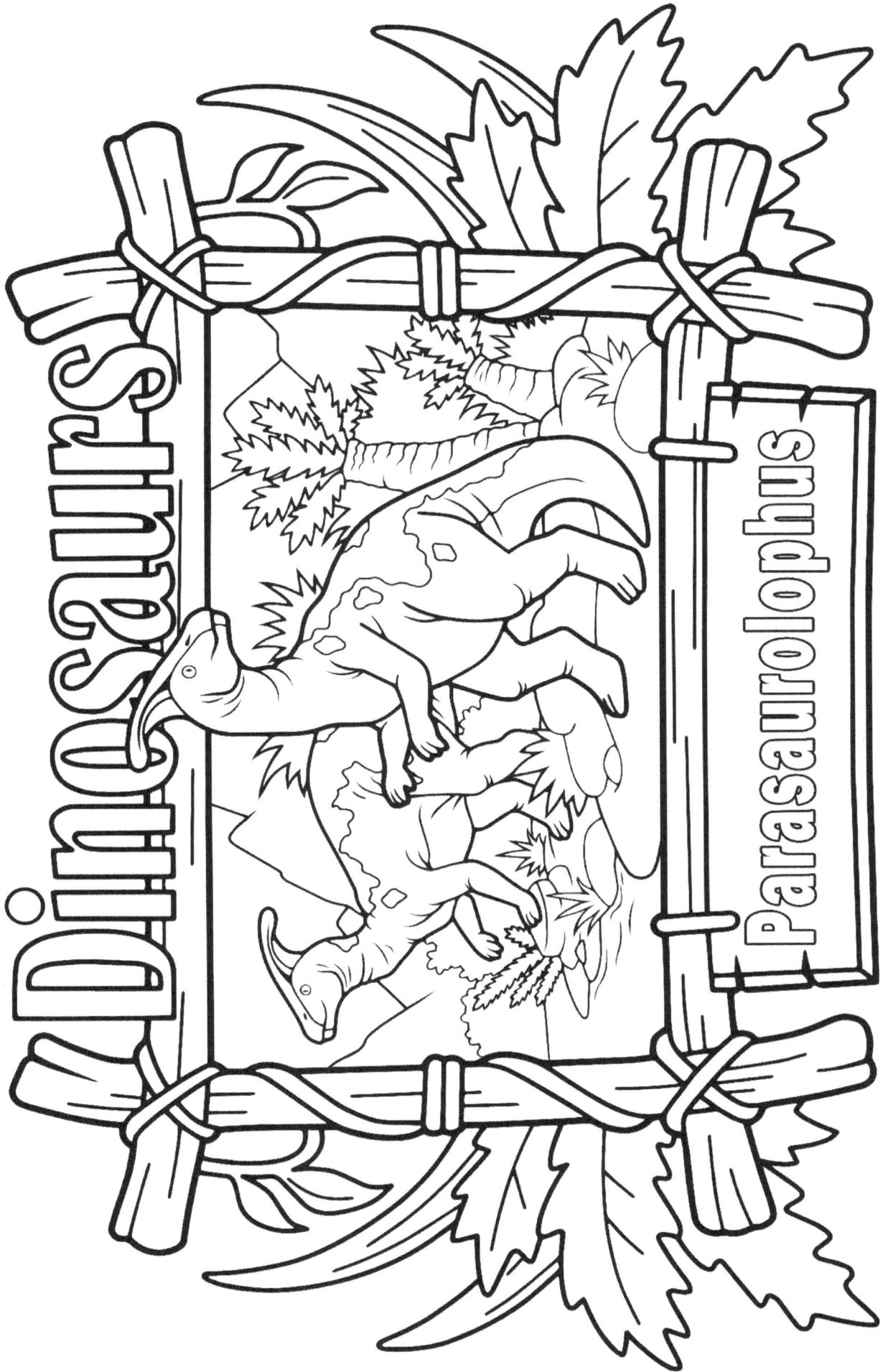

Dinosaurs

Parasaurolophus

OVIRAPTOR FACTS

Species Type	Oviraptor philoceratops **Dinosaur Type** Theropod
Movement	Stood and walked on its two slender back legs
Period	Late Cretaceous (about 99 to 65.5 million years ago)
Diet	Carnivore. Diet most likely consisted of fish and shellfish
Life Span	5 years
Dimensions	Grew to a length of about 1.8m (6 feet) and stood about 0.9m (3 feet) tall
Weight	About 70 pounds (32 kilograms)
Found in	Mainly in Asia, but some also have been found in North America
Miscellaneous	When scientists discovered Oviraptor it appeared to be lying on top of the eggs of another dinosaur. They named the dinosaur Oviraptor, which means "egg thief."

Dinosaurs

Oviraptor

CARCHARODONTOSAURUS FACTS

Species Type	Carcharodontosaurid Carnosaurs	**Dinosaur Type**	Theropod
Movement	Bipedal (walked on two legs)		
Period	Late Cretaceous period (99 – 65 million years ago)		
Diet	Carnivores.		
Life Span	Unknown		
Dimensions	About 13m (43 feet) long		
Weight	6 tons		
Found in	1924 in Algeria, Northern Africa		
Miscellaneous	Were able to lift animals weighing a maximum of 424 kg (935 lb) in its jaws based on the strength of its jaws, neck, and its center of mass. They reproduced by laying eggs.		

Dinosaurs

Carcharodontosaurus

SPINOSAURUS FACTS

Species Type	Spinosaurus Aegyptiacus	**Dinosaur Type**	Theropod
Movement	Bipedal (walked on two legs)		
Period	Cretaceous period (between 93 and 112 million years ago)		
Diet	Carnivore. A predator who ate meat		
Life Span	30 years		
Dimensions	Between 12.5m to 18m (41 to 59 feet)		
Weight	Between 7 to 23 tons		
Found in	Discovered in 1912 in Egypt, Africa		
Miscellaneous	The Spinosaurus is the largest carnivorous dinosaur known to exist. They had pressure sensors on its snout, just like an alligator, to detect potential prey moving in the water. They were able to swim.		

Dinosaurs

Spinosaurus

VELOCIRAPTOR FACTS

Species Type	Velociraptor Mongoliensis	**Dinosaur Type**	Small Theropod
Movement	Bipedal (walked on two legs)		
Period	Upper Cretaceous period (about 71 to 75 million years ago)		
Diet	Carnivore (meat eater!)		
Life Span	42 years		
Dimensions	Up to 1.8m (6.8 feet) in height		
Weight	81 kg (180 pounds)		
Found in	Discovered in 1923, in Outer Mongolian Gobi Desert, East Asia		
Miscellaneous	It is considered to be a bird-like dinosaur which comes from two Latin words meaning "speed" and "robber"! A formidable predator, with a large brain that contributed towards agility. Top speed of 40 mph, could reach 50 mph when hungry.		

Dinosaurs

Velociraptor

PLESIOSAURUS FACTS

Species Type	Plesiosaurus Dolichodeirus	**Dinosaur Type**	Plesiosauridae
Movement	Swimmer		
Period	Early to Middle Jurassic Period (135 to 120 million years ago)		
Diet	Carnivore. Living mostly on fish and belemnites		
Life Span	Unkown		
Dimensions	Around 3 to 5m (10 to 16 ft) in total length		
Weight	1,000 Pound (455 Kg)		
Found in	Discovered in 1823, in Western Europe		
Miscellaneous	Characterized by their long necks, sleek bodies, small heads and wide flippers. They had to come to shore to lay their eggs.		

Dinosaurs

Plesiosaurus

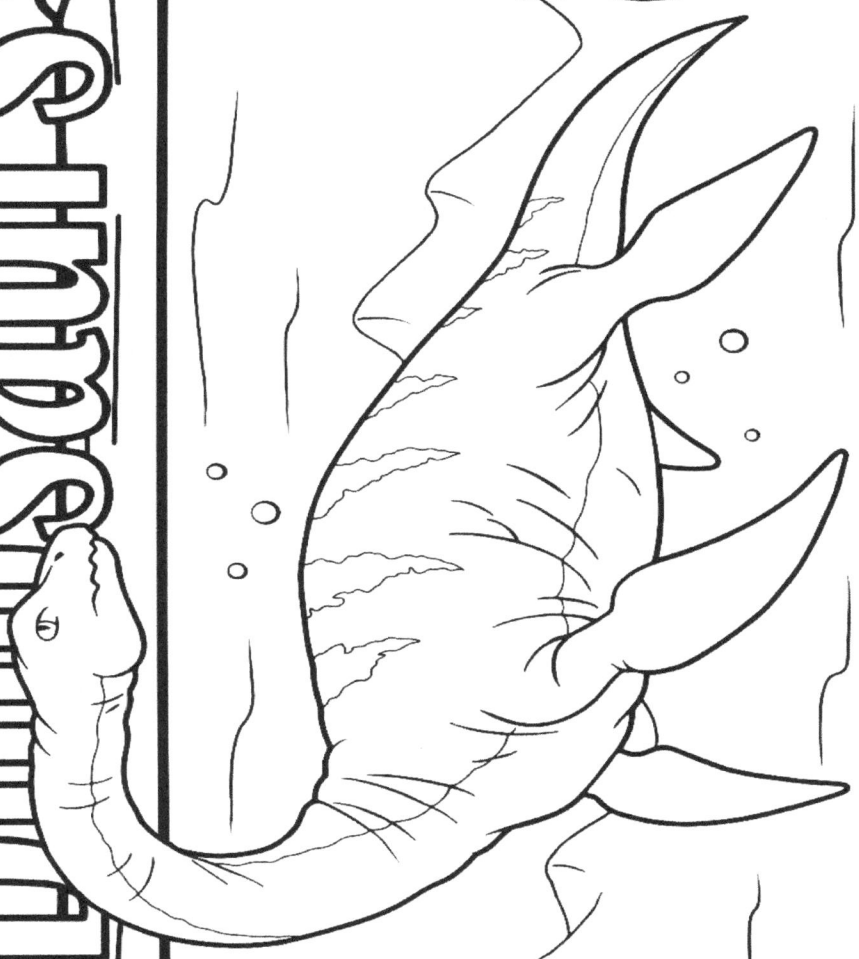

PACHYCEPHALOSAURUS FACTS

Species Type	Pachycephalosaurus Wyomingensis	**Dinosaur Type**	Pachycephalosauria
Movement	Bipedal (walked on two legs)		
Period	Late Cretaceous Period (between 66 and 72.1 million years ago)		
Diet	Herbivore. But teeth similar to carnivorous theropods		
Life Span	82 years		
Dimensions	4.5m (15 feet) in Length		
Weight	990 pounds (450 kg)		
Found in	Discovered between 1859 and 1860 in Montana, near Missouri River		
Miscellaneous	They had two arms with five-clawed fingers and two legs with three-clawed toes. A skull that is about 30 times thicker and stronger than a modern-day human skull. Reached a top speed of 34 mph.		

Dinosaurs

Pachycephalosaurus

LIOPLEURODON FACTS

Species Type	Thalassophonea	**Dinosaur Type**	Pliosauridae
Movement	Swimmer		
Period	Middle Jurassic Period (160 to 150 million years ago)		
Diet	Carnivore. Ate all what moved in the oceans.		
Life Span	Unknown		
Dimensions	Up to 9m (30 feet) in length		
Weight	2.5 ton (5,000 pounds)		
Found in	First discovered in 1873 near Boulogne-sur-Mer, France		
Miscellaneous	Its nostril arrangement means that it had a directional sense of smell. Could possibly swim as fast as a shark – which is about 25 miles per hour.		

Dinosaurs

Liopleurodon

LEPTOCERATOPS FACTS

Species Type	Leptoceratops Gracilis	**Dinosaur Type**	Ceratopsia
Movement	Quadrupedal (walked on four legs)		
Period	Upper Cretaceous Period (about 68–65 million years ago)		
Diet	Herbivore. Able to chew extremely tough plant matter		
Life Span	6 years		
Dimensions	Around 2m (6.6 feet) long		
Weight	Between 150 to 441 lb (68 to 200 kg)		
Found in	Discovered in 1910 in the Red Deer Valley in Alberta, Canada		
Miscellaneous	It had a large skull are there was a horn on its beaked snout. A 2016 study revealed that Leptoceratops was able to chew its food much like several groups of mammals.		

Dinosaurs!

leptoceratops

IGUANODON FACTS

Species Type	Iguanodon bernissartensis	**Dinosaur Type**	Ornithopod
Movement	Quadrupedal (walked on four legs) and bipedal (also on two legs)		
Period	Late Jurassic - Early Cretaceous (between 113 and 126 million years)		
Diet	Herbivore. Ate plants, and maybe fruits or seeds.		
Life Span	25+ years		
Dimensions	Between 9m and 13m (30 and 43 feet)		
Weight	3.5 tons		
Found in	Discovered in 1822. Lived in Europe (including England, Belgium and the Isle of White), but found also in Africa and North America.		
Miscellaneous	The top running speed of the Iguanodon is around 15 miles per hour. It is one of the best-known dinosaurs because it was one of the first dinosaurs ever to be described.		

Dinosaurs

Iguanodon

DIMETRODON FACTS

Species Type	Clepsydrops limbatus **Dinosaur Type** Tetrapod
Movement	Quadrupedal (walked on four legs)
Period	Cisuralian (Early Permian Period) (around 295–272 million years ago)
Diet	Carnivore, probably the top predator in its environment
Life Span	Unknown
Dimensions	1.7m to 4.6m (5.6 to 15.1 feet)
Weight	28 and 250 kilograms (62 and 551 lb)
Found in	In 1870, from the red beds in Texas and Oklahoma
Miscellaneous	It could warm up in the early morning by placing itself broadside to the Sun, and later could cool off in the shade, or arrange for its body to get less sunlight.

Dinosaurs

Dimetrodon

DILOPHOSAURUS FACTS

Species Type	Dilophosaurus Wetherilli	**Dinosaur Type**	Theropod
Movement	Bipedal (walked on two legs)		
Period	Early Jurassic (about 193 million years ago)		
Diet	Carnivore. Hunted dinosaurs as large as prosauropods		
Life Span	42 years		
Dimensions	Up to 7m (23 feet) in length		
Weight	Up to 400 kg (880 pounds)		
Found in	in 1940, in Navajo County, Arizona, USA.		
Miscellaneous	They had 16 teeth in its upper jaw and 17 in its lower jaw, and it could have eaten fish and other marine animals. In 2017, Connecticut designated it as their state dinosaur. 30 mph top speed.		

Dinosaurs

dilophosaurus

CERATOSAURUS FACTS

Species Type	Ceratosaurus Nasicornis **Dinosaur Type** Theropod
Movement	Bipedal (walked on two legs)
Period	Late Jurassic Period (between 156.3 and 146.8 million years ago)
Diet	Carnivore
Life Span	72 years
Dimensions	Up to 7m (23 feet) in length
Weight	Up to 952 kg (2,100 pounds)
Found in	Between 1883 and 1884, in Canon City, Colorado
Miscellaneous	Their teeth were so long that they extended past their bottom jaw when its mouth was closed. It is most recognizable by the two horns above its eyes and a horn in the middle of its snout. 18 - 31 mph top speed

Dinosaurs

CERATOSAURUS

BRACHIOSAURUS FACTS

Species Type	Brachiosaurus Altithorax **Dinosaur Type** Sauropod
Movement	Quadrupedal (walked on four legs)
Period	Late Jurassic period (between 153 and 154 million years ago)
Diet	Herbivore. Ate foliage at the top of tree canopies
Life Span	200 years
Dimensions	Between 18m and 21m (59 and 69 feet) in length
Weight	Between 28 and 62 tons
Found in	Discovered in 1900, in Colorado, USA
Miscellaneous	They ate between 400 and 900 pounds of food each day. They had no predators. The average size of an apex predator living during the same period would of only been half the size. Walk up to 5 mph.

Dinosaurs-First

brachiosaurus

BARYONYX FACTS

Species Type	Baryonyx Spenius Habiculum	**Dinosaur Type**	Theropod
Movement	Both quadrupedal and bipedal		
Period	Early Cretaceous period (about 130–125 million years ago)		
Diet	Carnivore. Diet consists mainly of fish		
Life Span	62 years		
Dimensions	9.5m (31 feet)		
Weight	1.2 tons		
Found in	Discovered in 1983 in the Weald Clay Formation of Surrey, England		
Miscellaneous	They're territorial and aggressive, living in flooded natural caves that are found along the river. they have a very good night vision that allows them to see in the darkness of their caves, which makes them formidable hunters. Could reach a top speed of 18 mph.		

Dinosaurs

Baryonyx

ANKYLOSAURUS FACTS

Species Type	Ankylosaurus Magniventris	**Dinosaur Type**	Thyreophora
Movement	Quadrupedal (walked on four legs)		
Period	Cretaceous Period (between 66 to 68 million years ago)		
Diet	Herbivore. Ate each day 170 kg of foliage near the ground		
Life Span	Between 70 and 80 years		
Dimensions	Between 6m and 8m (20 and 26 feet) in length		
Weight	Between 4 and 8 tons (9,000 to 17,500 pounds)		
Found in	1906, in the Hell Creek Formation, near Gilbert Creek, Montana		
Miscellaneous	They had a very good sense of smell. Their back had a lot of bony plates which would have protected them from the teeth of a predator. Paleontologist called it a living tank. Top speed of 6 mph.		

Dinosaurs

Ankylosaurus

ALLOSAURUS FACTS

Species Type	Allosaurus Fragilis
Dinosaur Type	Theropod
Movement	Bipedal (walked on two legs)
Period	Late Jurassic Period (between 150 and 155 million years ago)
Diet	Carnivore. They hunted large sauropods in a group
Life Span	72 years
Dimensions	9m (30 feet) in length and 4m (14 feet) in height
Weight	2 tons (4,600 pounds)
Found in	Discovered in 1877, in Colorado, USA
Miscellaneous	Allosaurus was the supreme predator during the end of the Jurassic, though it was somewhat overshadowed by T-Rex in Jurassic world. Designated the official state fossil of Utah in 1988. It reached 50 mph for short distances, 19 – 34 mph for long distances.

Dinosaurs

Allosaurus

SPINOSAURUS FACTS

Species Type	Spinosaurus Aegyptiacus	**Dinosaur Type**	Theropod
Movement	Bipedal (walked on two legs)		
Period	Cretaceous period (between 93 and 112 million years ago)		
Diet	Carnivore. Both semi-aquatic fish eaters and terrestrial hunters		
Life Span	30 years		
Dimensions	Between 12.5m and 18m (41 and 59 feet) in length		
Weight	Between 7 and 23 tons (15,500 and 51,000 pounds)		
Found in	Discovered in 1912 in Egypt, Northern Africa		
Miscellaneous	The Spinosaurus was an apex predator of its time, and it is the largest carnivorous dinosaur known to exist. The sail on its back helps it regulate its body temperature. Top speed of 25 mph.		

Dinosaurs

Spinosaurus

STYRACOSAURUS FACTS

Species Type	Styracosaurus Albertensis **Dinosaur Type** Ceratopsia
Movement	Quadrupedal (walked on four legs)
Period	Cretaceous Period (between 75 and 75.5 million years ago)
Diet	Herbivore. Ate a wide variety of vegetation near the ground
Life Span	40 years
Dimensions	5.5m (18 feet) in length
Weight	Around 3 tons (6,600 pounds)
Found in	Discovered in 1913 in the Dinosaur Park Formation in Alberta, Canada.
Miscellaneous	Very flexible omnivores, will eat a wide range of flora including grass, ferns, fruits and flowers. Their sharp beaks are very powerful, allowing them to crack open coconuts, melons and crush bone. 35 mph speed.

Dinosaurs

Styracosaurus

STEGOSAURUS FACTS

Species Type	Stegosaurus Stenops	**Dinosaur Type**	Thyreophora
Movement	Quadrupedal (walked on four legs)		
Period	Late Jurassic (between 150 and 155 million years ago)		
Diet	Herbivore. Ate a wide variety of vegetation near the ground		
Life Span	Between 75 and 100 years		
Dimensions	Up to 9m (29 feet) in length		
Weight	Between 5 to 7 tons (11,000 to 15,500 pounds)		
Found in	First discovered in 1877, in north of Morriso, Colorado, USA.		
Miscellaneous	The state dinosaur of Colorado. Its brain was the size of a walnut. It wasn't an easy meal for predators, as the plates on its back and spiked tail were an excellent way to defend against predators. 30 mph top speed.		

Dinosaurs

Stegosaurus

TRICERATOPS FACTS

Species Type	Ceratops Horridus	**Dinosaur Type**	Ceratopsid
Movement	Quadrupedal (walked on four legs)		
Period	Late Cretaceous Period (around 65 million years ago)		
Diet	Herbivore. Biting off plant material with its beak and processing it with its tooth batteries		
Life Span	40 years		
Dimensions	Could reach up to 9m (30 feet) in length and 3m (10 feet) in height		
Weight	Between 6.5 to 13 tons (Roughly the size of an elephant)		
Found in	Discovered in 1887, near Denver, Colorado, USA.		
Miscellaneous	It's name means "Three Horned Face". It doesn't stand much of a chance against an attack from the back and from both sides should it be unlucky enough. Reached a top speed of 35 mph.		

Dinosaurs

Triceratops

Made in the USA
Las Vegas, NV
17 February 2021

18085884R00033